Tammy Stone

FORMATION

Along the Ganges and Back Again

Acknowledgements:

Everything exists in relationship, and I could not have arrived at this book without the help and support of so many. I'd like to thank Glenn Lyvers and Prolific Press for taking this leap with me, and working tirelessly to bring this collection to life, as well as April Zipser for proofreading the manuscript. I'd like to thank the beautiful people of Nong Khai, a home away from home, and Beatrix Schilcher, Pancho and Suzy Fraser for their teachings and profound inspiration. Thank you to my parents, Peter and Rosa Stone, and my sister and brother-in-law, Debbie and Mike Feierstein, for keeping me close as I've travelled so far. Thank you to the dear ones I've met during my travels, who have housed and taught me, shared in the journey, and offered kindnesses beyond description. Takeshi Takahashi, my love, thank you for being the space between words.

Some chapter poems that appear in this book, all untitled, previously appeared in the following journals, to whom I would also like to express my deep gratitude: The Camel Saloon (Sep. 20, 2011, Aug. 16, 2013); The Bamboo Forest; Orion headless (Aug. 24, 2011); Dairy River (Vol. 11, Dec. 2013), and Buddhist Poetry Review (Issue Eight, Spring 2013).

FORMATION

Along the Ganges and Back Again

Tammy Stone

Contents:

For Takeshi

It Came From Here

It should always be
Sunday morning
with pancakes
cocoa and my
mother's love.

What did I used to make
out of toilet paper rolls,
        except for the whole universe?
There were egg cartons too,
and the skins of grapefruit
shelled in early morning,
those yellow-domed testaments to the dreams
that made me.

When you're little
the world outside your house is magic,
hardly there.

~~~OOO~~~

"Come outside.
        There's new dandelions,"
I say to my sister.
She's watching
The Flintstones
        on our sea-blue carpet
which covers the living / dining
room and hallway. It's a small house;
we call it *The Lollipop House*
because it looks like a circle
on top of a stick, *but*
sideways. My sister's room
is shades of orange and brown
and mine is a few kinds of green.
She's watching
The Flintstones,
        because that's what's on
our brand new color TV.
She's ignoring me.
Earlier this morning
I agreed to play
Candy Land with her
but she cheated
        again
so I called her a Big Fat Cheater
and calmly got up
and left the room.
She threw the board game
        at me
but it didn't get far

enough, and then she started
to yell and cry. A few days ago,
my mother was teaching me to
braid using hair ribbons
tied to the dining room chair
and my sister snuck up
        from behind
and pinched my shoulder
really hard
and
ran away. My mother said,
"You come back here this instant
and apologize.
        I mean it!" My sister ran
back to the living room / dining room
and said, "Fine. Sorry."
But she obviously
didn't mean it.

Barry Manilow is playing on the stereo
because my mother loves Barry Manilow.
Before I was born, she also loved
The Beatles
        but now we don't have any Beatles
albums in the house.
I don't wonder why though
because I don't know
anything about it.
Last year my best
friend's parents took
my best friend, me and my sister to see
the *Miq et Miquettes* play
because they are rising stars in Montreal.

But my sister
ate too many chips 'n dip
and she threw up mayonnaise so
we had to go home early.
Three years ago, we went to Walt Disney World,
        Florida
and my sister threw up in the spinning teacups
but I didn't. She
waited with my mother
while my dad and I went
on the Space Mountain ride
because she wasn't old enough.
It was so scary and exciting. I felt like I was
a different person when I came back
to the real world. Or maybe the world
was different because now it included outer space.
At the Disney store
we got to choose a present
        and I let my sister choose
first and she chose my favorite:
Donald Duck. So I chose
one of the Three Little Pigs.
In the future, I'll knit it a scarf
because my grandmother teaches me how
before her fingers get too arthritic.
She made us so many
matching clothes.
When my sister was one
        and I was two
she would try to talk but only I could
understand her. When she was a baby
I would take her bottle from her
and steal dolls from her crib

even though I never liked dolls.
She loved dolls, and she still loves them.
I told her she could bring them outside
but she still won't come
play with me.

There was a day
at the pool near our house
that was safe and predator free.
It was not a day for drowning.
My friend dove in-
to the shallow
end of the pool at Chamberlain Park,
a name I don't forget that spells sun and happy
rusted swings,
and hit her head on the bottom.
No one but me even noticed.
Time did not stand still
and anyway,
I didn't know time.
I certainly didn't know death.
I watched her hit bottom.

She was down there
for maybe three seconds
before coming back up.
"Ouch," she said, and rubbed her scalp
with a pruned hand.

Our mothers were minding our little sisters,
who needed minding more.
There's a photo of us—
who grew up together
behind the knees of our parents,
the kids of high school love,
on a sunny afternoon, barbeque
with watermelon, margarine-slabbed corn,
dads laughing, wives kicking back.
There are bright fizzy TV colors
and the flat solid white of Casper—
The Friendly Ghost,
big chunky jewelry
and short curly mom-hair,
and floral paintings
on pastel walls.

We used to put on plays
in my friend's basement
with our sisters
while our parents
chatted over coffee
and layer cake.
She and I were
the shy ones.
But when we performed together
we ruled the world,

we created it.
In the photo of our families,

we're both flexing our feet,
our legs are stiff

we're both locked somewhere
deep inside ourselves,
        but there's that gleam in our eye.
Years later, she hit her head again,
just an accident, really,
but the concussion initially covered up how
she lost her short term memory,
        which left her
everything she had before the accident,
and pleasant smiles for everything that came after.

~~~OOO~~~

I don't talk on the phone anymore.
The phone is still
installed, sits on a chair I found
at the back of a Mexican restaurant,
an iron, backless chair with
a turquoise leather cushion. It gathers
dust I never remove. The alleyway
at the back of the restaurant, where I walk
once a week, is full
of concrete
and the colors of dead,
regal things. Wires and electrical ditties
sprout everywhere, from porous brick
walls to the cavernous bottoms of doorways
and crown molding like veins
that pulse
the sun itself.
Some are cut and hang limp

without this kind of life in it
and when I see these sprigs
of former circuitry,
I think the city
must have died, and I mourn
this, because I love my city.
          (I know, though,
that in a dead city there is no room for phone calls.)
I sigh. A bird comes
to sit on the windowsill, the one in the kitchen
with its yellow walls
and dried out spices.

I don't use my spices anymore
because once my eyes started swelling
at everything I saw
outside walking,
I realized there was no smell or taste
anymore. My eyes have become wide
gaping receptacles,
and the world knows all about it.
I'm sure of this. The world flocks to me
because it thinks
I've been waiting to see. Every color and shape
pounces, like a movie, until I need to scream,
and dance them out,
until there's nothing left inside
that is originally my own.
The bird that sits on my window
wants to poke me until I bleed
the city back into life.
It works *(or the rest would not follow).*

~~~OOO~~~

I miss waking
screaming in the night.
One day I'm walking home from work
when
I know:
     My childhood is gone.
How does something like that go
missing and how do you get it back?
I call my mother
and ask her
to tell me things.

She tells me what I know,
but I need it again.
It bears its message in
her soft, fervent elocution,
and pads my heart for
what will come:
I was shy, we were happy,
yes and I didn't make trouble.
Like a keepsake
we exchange through the seasons,
the love that carries through.

It Starts With Dreams

Tell yourself to me,
I'm tired of your words.
Give me your pen
and look for me
        (in my eyes), speak your madness there.
I'll hold onto its structure
like it is a beating
heart itself.
I understand that

there are words and pictures, I know
that they can bring tears and fill the chest
with how
love moves.

What is there in saying all this?

Images remain,
        the bearer of the words
transmigrates, once
here and now in a place
from which no voices carry
with them the promise of utterance.
What is not
has passed another way.
Forever
means little to the dead,
words don't speak
to those who have once lived.
When the world wakes up

it will find a tangle
in incomprehensible phrasing,
and will discover
in them an abstract beauty that says don't touch,
and will play with them anyway,
to decipher their meaning.
The origin of the words was hope
for new articulation.

Hear the words now
before all words turn to fossil,
turn to litter, turn
to a new kind of floating gold.

I'm tired.
This brings an ease,
we remember to smile:
        the body does.
We're at the lush green place with coconut
in the middle
and the pressure
to will a feeling disappears. We just look at it
and it's pretty,
touch it
where the spirit moves,
        even if we can't
it's okay,
because what is a tree?
What is green, or mountain, or lush view?

So you laugh,
we hear it in the wind between us.

One time I was so tired
everything looked red,
not because I couldn't sleep
for holy-numbered nights feeding a newborn
        or being plagued by nightmares.
I love sleep, the dreams that come,

the engulfing darkness.

Like we get to be in the shadow of a mountain,
emboldened and subsumed.
I suppose, waiting.

I dream and a person comes,
a very old man wearing coveralls
and a straw hat.
His beard has the air of whiskers,
making him look a little like Lao Tzu.
He doesn't say anything
for the longest time. He regards me with gentle eyes,
eventually holding out
his ancient hand. There's a toothpick
in his mouth, which he's chewed to bits.
I don't know
I'm dreaming
but usually I'm hesitant and anxious

in dreams;
now I take his hand
without thought.
As soon as I do,
we're sitting
under a tree in a small field
and a river flows by
alongside us hiding
a strong current that has caused many deaths
and as soon as this thought strikes me,
it's clear I'm in Laos,
which is where I am
for real,
though in my dream I'm back home
in Canada, being led by this old man
to the northern Southeast
Asian mountains,
just south of where most of the unexploded
ordnance was dropped
during the war.
Now a rainbow
appears, a luminous band
I can see
in its entirety:
my first full rainbow.
The old man is taking it in
with a slow smile and steady gaze.
He's Jack Kerouac,
calmer, past the struggles,
        still in love with the road.
"Beautiful, isn't it," he says.
"Now go back to your loving husband,
and get yourself some sleep."

"Funny," I say. I leave the dream and love
my husband, and watch the sun feed the river.
Sometimes I still try to enter sleep awake
so I can find Jack Kerouac Lao Tzu again,
but sleep isn't a shiny light
bouncing here and there
on the clear plains. Sleep is a story
between what you know
and what your dreams are for.

I want that tree over there
to talk to
me. Or any tree.
This is just
the one I can see right now,
a big mango tree
and they've carved a courtyard in-
to the space around it, filled with big stones
that were embedded before the concrete,
dried so you can walk on it
and it's like an earth-
sized massage
for the feet.

They also help create friction so you don't slip
when the floor gets wet,
which is often
because there's a vat of water in the corner
you use to splash

cold water on yourself
before going into the sauna,
so hot it feels like walking into fire.
Or taking a test-
run of hell, if such a thing exists.
You sit down
and the fire hurls itself in-
to your nostrils.
You stand up
and the flames engorge your head.
You make a run for it
and the curtain rips your skin off.

There's little space between these
activities
to simply sweat
the toxins out.
But in the courtyard,
there are endless refills of bael fruit tea.
And the mango tree reminds me
how much I want
the trees
to talk
to me.

I guess trees are like those who are watching.
Flowers are precious
but they don't live long.
Ants too,
they run around working together
and carry their sustenance,
but, though they see
a universe in miles,

they don't know
what I've learned
in time, from my own lowly position in the scheme
of things, while many-ringed
trees have lived many-ringed lives,
          seen what changes.
Sometimes I take bus rides to visit my parents
in my hometown, where change doesn't
announce itself.

Then the old gas station
at the corner across the Loeb
has been replaced
by a Shell,
and the butcher has become an Asian
fusion-restaurant,
and even though the old Quickie
has never even had a paint job,
there is that
unshakeable feeling that there is no stopping time.
Which means I have become one who watches,
like trees,
even as they make fruit
and unfold with the seasons.
"You like tree."
It's the Lao woman who gave me a sarong
for the sauna.
"Yes," I say.
"Trees have spirit," she says.
"Here. You put cream on skin.
Good for you. Make young again."

From Here, I See

Of all the days spent
doing the littlest things
I love you the most.

One drop sounds,
I see a kitchen sink
spotted in light,
maybe a live-in nanny or a partner
to whom I have given my love.
He fixes the sink
that otherwise gleams
in speckled hues; he holds the new juicer
that yesterday made something
with kale and lime,
even in this vision, I am
back in Asia,
          not knowing why
this is what compelled me.
Who resembles the person
I write about?
The sound of one drop
means the water of the world has heard me,
this is a necessity
as it is inevitable.
I don't want to be
obtuse, or even coherent.

I want to imagine
the kitchen with the juicer.
I want to one day have one with the man
to whom I
have given my love. *Eat the tree*
to be a tree,
someone might say
through the fog,
it must be a deity,
and now I'm in a forest,
late afternoon, or maybe it's pre-dawn,
I am feral
with lucid white skin,

I am unable to be tamed.
My eyes have seen.
Yet the seahorses and exotic fruits
surround me still, still born, wild made,
this has nothing to do with me,
come back,
it's so simple.
Find a swing to swing on.
Sing for forgiveness.
But come back to me.

~~~OOO~~~

See the distant scream, the belly full
of emotions sapped from lime,
from the mountain I found last year
with the Name that was freely given.

I can watch,
gauge the silence
for its potential wrath,
find the sadness I puncture to dispel,
from the mountaintop
where the air is thin
the space between points distilled and ready,
come play, for us, like
when we used our mothers'
sewing shears
to cut pieces
of wrapping paper
for our shoebox dollhouses.
It was bright and transparent,
however it turned out.
Our hearts too, we wished for love
the way we moved through gauzy curtains
far from where our dreams sing dark to the ground.

We did not know
of the Indian palaces yet.
        But the dreams
were the same.
        They were so close,
our joy and heart.
        They giggled, waiting,

dreams are meant to invite us back to ourselves.
Let's visit the palaces,
        make an offering of our childhood
creations, watch
our emotions race up to join the others.
Can we breathe together

in this way? Dance
in purple delight, silk and velvet
creatures of the night.

They say it's science,
that time is moving
to a vanishing
point,

ever faster, even as it never was, so that
its disappearance
invites beautiful things
on the other side of irony and disappointment.
But, I don't think
of these things now,
because there is a candle
flickering on
the wooden table,
and a tea I'm brewing,
and crickets sounding the sill.

A coiled display
of violet and white flowers.
Eden with her vision, this is our house
behind it, couched

in a secret
garden cut from a picture book
construction, old furniture
neatly folded in-
to square piles underneath, another house
at the end of the lot, two wooden structures
not speaking,
two cats belonging to a third house
across the street, visiting where the love is.
        Time does not mark itself
in perfection. Fill the space with opera,
with bloated movie soundtracks.
The silence between hears us,
or the tortured sounds of mangy dogs
limping down the road,
who can also be the coyotes of a dry desert
sending messages into the saddest moon,
and then the clink
of a coffee cup in a roadside diner
somewhere in a neon place
insulated from all this.

I never knew this at all. Sometimes it's best to stop
between the desert and the secret garden;
they create a battle for the heart in one body.

To come awake,
the start of what I need
to say to you.

It's been a long time now
that I have been taken in by things
we didn't ever know,
the flare of dragons'
nostrils as they jump up and down,
absent from our mythology,
engaging in mock flight.
Now, the carvings on temples,
the costumed Bali evenings,
and the sun has put away
its fire again.
And again, we climb,
you are so beautiful
in the way of the warriors.
Also on temple doors,
dancing lithe and strong,
how you have
let your beauty out,
and sometimes I think of how we used to envision
our future
next door houses.

Now I walk on
temple grounds, far away
from where you are,
        and I see you everywhere—
etched on gilded walls—
I walk quietly along,
touching the textured wood,
the crackling paint,
hiding in the darkness
when I need to, and lighter
things too, washing in the

Andaman Sea, discovering
flight in song
and how have we not
talked about love?
Let's greet it together,
         this place for stories.
I made so many
choices on my own.
I don't know yours.
Even the magic, then,
and it has been so abundant,
is only a part of it.

When they smile,
it's like a new world
pushing in from somewhere close;
we've seen it, I'm sure,
this smile is more a reminder
than an awakening, though
every part of me now breathes
new and it's never been
another way. You know
when something refuses
to leave without
that trace.

It's not just one smile.
It's everywhere you look while the rest comes
and goes as we watch. I watch for hours

in the garden restaurant, the cat purring
against a glossy vase to the tune of Lao pop.
Fix your eyes on the smiles and the gleaming white,
there's no better entry.
Mountains tower just beyond,
but right now, in this moment,
they edge
away as I eat, feet on rough sand.

The mountains I have tried to climb
holding the sacred close.
Those mountains will take you
to ever-after places.

The purity of a smile, so that
every time I see one here,
it is also a sun-glinted
memory.

Love says don't collapse;
it asks why fall now,
when all the dirt-lined pavements in the world
were carved from the purest stone for you?
This is not just the imagination,
        I don't think;
remember when I used to
predict the in-colors for the coming
season? The last one I remember
talking about was purple, it was

probably the late eighties,
and I didn't like purple
at all.

Now I wear a purple shawl
laced with thin silver strands;
there's an intricate image on it
in darker purple.
I think it's a cosmic flower sheltering
smaller buds.

I don't know if I came
to like the color
or if we just found each other somehow,
        past the time of strong affinities
or dislikes
or building ourselves.

Maybe it's that I fail to confront what I see,
or beauties merge,
but somehow love appears stronger,
more diffuse.
The sun lowers in the sky
and the world is light.
It loves to be loved, love,
and it doesn't ask that we leap
off tall buildings or cry as much as that,
to find it. A pretty stone carving
isn't made in a day,
but it doesn't take forever either.
We are all in between,
aren't we? Like the years we passed together,
before we said goodbye.

To observe, to measure,
to stand apart, how
many years spent in this way,
serving distance,
feeding my mind's divergences;
at the same time,
I am after the rainbow's way,
grateful for its qualities.

I don't want to be apart
anymore. But the rainbow
is meant for this,
for passing through,
while we concern ourselves
with a state of being in,
fearing so much. I've never seen a rainbow
up close, or tried to get inside,
and don't actually know about the possibilities
of this. Maybe one can get inside of anything.

I watched a man feed monkeys this morning.
He's probably been doing this for years.
The monkeys aren't afraid to come
close; they're used to people here.
But there was no friendly exchange
between man and monkey.
He was a hand reaching out
with half a banana. The monkeys would stare
for a long time, not knowing what or whom to
trust. They'd look around, furtively, unsure.

Then, with a quick snap, they'd grab
the food, look around again
with quick eyes,
and run off
to eat — a
fight-to-the-end affair
together with their clan,
but also alone. I have
tried to stand apart
and am relieved now
to have failed
as I have.

Servitude.
To serve one who is serving someone or something
else. When we can't see the source, we can
serve it anyway. This is the foundation of faith,
or maybe its definition.
I used to think
having faith meant being blind and I misunderstood
blindness. There are things we shouldn't see
if we want to aim for happiness.
Not a turning away from,
but a moving to what is,
instead, an embracing.

I want to accept
        to be accepting.
I want to be blind to certain distinctions

(or becoming is impossible). Sri Ramana Maharshi's
cave, where he sat in for fifty years,
inspires these words. I woke up
sad today, and walking to the cave was hard.
Now I can look down the mountain and see
that I live here now, down there in those dusty,
rocky plains, and not some other there, or
then. It comes to me that sadness has a history,
it isn't now. Sadness takes you back,
brings you memories to anchor it, terrifies you
in the dark, because of who you were and might
still be. Saying goodbye to sadness should be
as easy as leaving the last decade,
not thinking in memories,
which we do as we breathe, happily,
in a different kind of light.

I hear you loudest
in the song coming faintly
from somewhere else in this new city,
this early morning, the sun
has just risen but it's
nowhere to be found.
I can't guess at the
source of the sound yet,
just that it's a shrill
but beautiful female
voice and it carries
all the way here where

shopkeepers are starting
their day quietly
and together. Always
together, like a song.
How many times did
the music remake itself
before coming to these incensed airwaves,
these times, who tried to
make it perfect? Now it is fixed in sharp-sweet
melody. Close to
me bare feet resonate loudly on pebbles,
European-inspired alleys
and the metallic floors of bright yellow
transportation. You have
come so far with me,
hiding in the sun.

Its expression, walking in the dark
under glowing stars
which can't get too close together or
they collide and I can
remember a time when
all the world's
flowers disappeared,
and returned again.
I can't forget the colors on the leaves
and how they formed
such intricate patterns, like tablecloths
and the wallpaper of our youth.

These colors were going nowhere,
they were defiant
and they almost overtook.
Then something changes,
and the flowers are gone
and even the joy I find in speaking to you,
here,
evades
me. Not because of what's been lost,
but because of how life is, how one can have
slipped without any awareness of getting
here. I don't want to talk about rabbit
holes. I just want to be
with the salty ocean wind.
And there's no trick-start, is there? I will
not fight with you again. I will not fight.
I will sing in the sun and photograph sunbeams
on walls
and if you see me I'll be smiling.

My teeth are still a little too big for my face
and when I smile it's all I can feel in my body.
I will be counting my breath and whispering
in gratitude for the space we're in. I will not
churn at the loose skirts and billowing shirts
imprinting the morning, or ignore the hello's of
those who evoke every single last mystery
far past the hole in the center of the earth,
the other side of which
– can you hear it?

~~~OOO~~~

We know the parameter of words,
but you are not here and I need to talk to you.
My heart's beating too fast. The sand is too hot.
If I slow down and watch this happen
the tears will start
and I don't want this.
The day was so perfect. It rained last night and
by the time we were up the sun was overhead.
I could see
this through a small patch of palm trees,
mingling for some time now, a harmonic-
triage of blue, green and yellow.
These are the symmetries
of early morning, the
sunflowers in the perfect sky.
        So there was promise.

I'm still in the future
        somewhere,
even as I write this to you. It only makes sense
now that the day has come to this, loveless,
around the corner
from hope. Even as I sit on the sand
and even as the sea sounds
like mounds of life forever
washing up on the shore. I am not what I am.
Do you have a horizon
like this too?

I never thought
about beauty this way, it not being nothing
           as naked form.
I just came back from a temple,
maybe the hundredth,
and it was so beautiful I couldn't breathe.
I realized that
beauty tells a vivid story past adornment
and the expression of passion or desire.
It does not just speak to that which
hopes to carry us
beyond suggestion.
Beauty is more than a tribute to the lure that has
inspired all religion. It is religion itself.
It is the blood that inspires, creates, and above all
loves, echoing through the architects, designers,
artisans and builders who make it.
I saw that beauty arises,
is not personification.
Beauty is what made us,
           and what we have made.

Something changes, wants to help me
more now, to gather and absorb knowledge
but not enfold me wildly into all this.

I think about education
and years of talking in confidence
to the words on the page
engaging in impassioned discourse,
which called to me its own end.

My body rejected knowledge.
I couldn't read,
my desires became unmoored.
I learned about love and fear
and I'm making so many mistakes.

Of course, love is not something you learn,
you do it,
like the little kids
singing a hymn,
the morning chant
whipping through
their pink and white uniforms
as they stand outside
the front entrance of their white
hillside school
as close as can be to the clear sun,
because we're in
the mountains now, and the teacher
will fill their bright heads
with curious things,
and satisfy their clever, impish imaginations,

but I'm more interested in
the school grounds,
a building not much bigger than a house,
with a corrugated iron roof and a

smaller room higher up,
just behind.

At the chai shop I sip sweet tea
by the paved road landing
where rickshaws carry new arrivals,
up the gothic, rounded stone
steps leading to roughly hewn benches for
morning gatherers and meditators,
reminding me of turrets
and golden tresses, and lairs and chivalry.

Uphill, past the moat without a castle
and school without a parking lot, the
forest. Cedars and pines,
the origin of green
and the source of everything
my mind now longs to know.
A song in the air around me says,
in the holy name of Shiva,
may you learn what
it is that haunts you,
because you and the world
are already such old companions,
and have shared so much.

~~~OOO~~~

And from the fort a city in re-awakening,
Jaisalmer, that mystery in gold
sparkling things set in sky and stone.

They form a clustered totality

around edges, gaps and
empty spaces,
you see
how nothing sticks,

how little can congeal,
already being at such great distance,
dreaming itself of mystics and ocean ends.
        Vegas and Elvis,
Toronto and late morning brunch,
they fly through time for me
unbroken and forward-bent,
and why not now, under a blinding sky.
Little birds sit on thickets of wire
a hop away from
a structure a thousand
years old.
You can't weave this where I'm from.
There, smells are newer too,
in refuse and legacy,
though I see us join hands
thrashing in the night begging for our return.
Here, I am captured:

the people who have roots
growing down,
I'm sure I have seen it.
I turn to the mark I've made on sandal-
flattened soil,
the growth of land and home.
The past is a bloody and transcendent

movement into today's
tailor shops, altars and saloons.

I don't want to romanticize
what I came from remote places to find.
But there is a feeling
that erupts so rarely now,
despite years of eastward time,
of having fallen somewhere deep
into the cracks and
folds of this long Earth,
which won't swallow
me up no matter
how much I implore

(my eyes are always seeking
the horizon).

So I glide under the weight of a few glimpses
and some laughing steps
and I can confirm again
what I have been slow to grasp about magic.

I have no doubt that it moves through
living things
(this is the Land
of Kings we found),
that it is here,
where I am. The clouds
glide toward the setting sun in answer.

The ground was wise not to
swallow me into its ancient rotation,

and the trees, of course,
have not moved near or far.
I am older but things fly off me now,
it's startling, and you,
the finest piece, my
queen of dreams,
the cities we've built,
the mirrors we've slid way
up into the galaxies
for the sole purpose there ever was,
and then it did,
love found us.

Kali Dance: Five Rupee Poems

Leaves in dust piles need to be swept,
an iron table rusting, waiting for use
so we bring our papaya,
cut it in half with a spoon,
walk around looking for somewhere to sit
and find ourselves on an old cremation ground.
We eat among the souls of the dead,
their songs holding up the sun.

"Is this your fortune,
to find this?"
I write on a napkin.
"It is also my fortune,
to write it for you."

There is a circle.
I'm sure you've seen it.
"The circle of life."
This is how it works.
All you have to do
is jump in at any point and start walking.
I'd love to know how it goes.

At the altar of someone
else's ancestors
I see Father, Grandfather,
I join in, I spend time with
their images.
I enter a family in this way,
I have chosen to belong here.

Be a queen, not a princess,
he says over tea.
His white clothes hang
on his lean body.
There's a breeze
and the sun is hiding.
We sit on red plastic chairs.
He says, princesses need
too much.
Queens already have everything.

My *guru*, the young
student seeker says,
as he gives us
a photo mounted
on the wall of a tiny cave
sitting on the extended mountain peak.
From his small home,
in loose orange clothes,
he offers us cookies,
an almond each,
and chai served
in half a coconut shell.

Buses leaving
beggars begging
music thumping
colors popping
sarees swaying
talkers talking
mothers holding
we sit
sitters sitting
ground holding us
crumbling.

From inside the house,
I watch through the window.
A neighbor
steps outside
where it's bright,
bends
down
and takes the Earth
in his hands.
I know he's smiling.
The flowers are shining
and the trees
next to him
bend to the sun.

A pink circle
lights us today,
in our wanderings
around. Three waters
come calling
for a meeting, a gathering
of friends hosted
by rocks
of Land's End.

The sun rises again
in perfect geometry,
without rays,
says to the mist
and the clouds:
my friendly companions,
you have come
with me
all this way
all these years,
let's sit now
and wonder
about so-called mystery.

From 1940s Hungary
to 1980s Montreal
to 2000s India,
from grandmother's migrations
to granddaughter's own,
we share,
together
in places,
cake and tea with milk,
we drink
from glass cups,
she and I,

she always did but
I'm only beginning,
savoring the sweetness,
the ochre-
hot afternoon.

A woman in a saree
walks along the shore,
dogs play-fight and whip up sand,
a man sits on a towel
stretching and
watching the ocean
be the ocean.

Kollam, a place unknown to me.
We stumble out of a bus early morning,
I sit with heaps of onions waiting
for a room to be found for us.
They say it is home to a history of
Christian, Jewish, Muslim settlement
and is the world's largest
hub of the cashew nut.
Or maybe that's somewhere else
close by, though I've seen Jesus-
iconography everywhere.

The synagogue I thought I found
turned out to be a theatre.

Be aware
breath is waiting
for you to notice,
catch it so that time can announce
mystic realities,
like creatures people might wait
a lifetime to see under water.

If everyone is here for one reason,
inside the chamber of singing sounds,
if I notice, suddenly,
that the poison in the air
is gone,
and my heart is so still,
showing me its greatest wish,
what is there
before the next sounds come -
        an answer
makes new covers
for silence.

She smiles, eyes fixed in perfect concern
and no personal carriage,
there is joy
and sorrow
hands touching a head,
holding a shoulder
watching a heart in its rhythm

and she vanquishes
such heavy things
by showing
what they are.

A parasite vine
has crawled up the tower of an old tree,
sucking its life juices. *Ojas.*
They unite,
centuries of suckling
history,
vast eras of witness,
a jungle of wide green leaves
having their turn
in today's person-
place spectrum.

The dust spits at me
        and leaves,
making shadows.
A woman arrives,
the sand is hot,
she beams
golden-eyed
and the world glows,
she blows secrets at me,
what's past is
gone.

I'll stand forever
for one who knows,
glimpsing a starlit view,
strings of light across the water.
It's not far.
If I stand and take it in,
if I can feel the smile,
someone
        out there in
that orange parade
can find me.

~~~OOO~~~

This tree must be
as wide as a grandfather's ancestral years.
They've put strings around it
a tin can shrine out front,
decorated it with holy paints and
colored sands.
You can hear songs singing in it.
We take our time over ginger tea
saucers like the moon,
talk about mournful Japanese movies,
and only stop when we make the mistake
of thinking
it's time to go.

~~~OOO~~~

A pause:

      nothing more to say.

"Take it," I hear.
"It doesn't last.
Enter it.
Breathe until
it takes shape,
touches your skin."
Smiles widen
the she of things.

~~~OOO~~~

The wind is a story
from the oral tradition,
a Banyan like my wise grandmother, branching out
in cradling symmetries,
rocks
like visitors
from another planet.
We imbue them with these things
and deny ourselves
the heritage of our beauty.

~~~OOO~~~

You can
fill your body
over again

and there she is,
chanting songs,
psalms,
rows of people behind her,

pushing,

thrusting for you,
throwing the pink flower
over -

Opening my eyes
on the beach
in the sand
I saw gold dust first.
They make the shine
in secret when no-one's looking,
leaving form
and bounding together,
  moving
    freeform,
      going in
        for the deep swim.

Pretty girls in jeans
on cell phones
black hair shining
next to a man with
movie star hair
sitting on a motorbike
taking the attention
with a wink,
Mumbaikars in wait
- cameras get-set-roll.

Sugar cane juice boys
started smiling
before we arrived,
this is the third day now,
huge white teeth
gentle eyes light up with excitement,
photo! a snap! I can't resist I'm in love,
they pour sweet juice into our cups
for 10 rupees, and our
happiness is free.

Someone comes by
looking for a seat,
faces a large family sitting
with their luggage
and a potted plant not yet bloomed.
They invite him in.
There's one hook for his bag
and just enough room
if they squeeze.
Chatter resumes,
chapatti shared when the food comes out,
the train moves north,
sleeping room for everyone.

I look for treasures
on the ground, now in Delhi,
soiled cloth here and there,
a few pieces of scrap metal
not even the scavengers
can find use for,
dusty and soiled
leftovers, humming shards
of bright life.

To feel what I know,
to expand what I feel
so I might understand
the emotions that flow in and through
in mutable exchange,
like the birds roaming
through the mountain-
facing window.

"I came here from Tibet
in 2005."
"I came to Dharamsala

when I was 13."
Words and smiles
flush with warmth
over thenthuk at the Momo Café,
two-way curiosity amid
bewildering circumstances:
essence of wonder.

The dogs' spacious home
wide as the world
a geometry of visitors
and temporary lodgings.
They hobble over to our bed on injured legs
appearing playful,
immediately rolling onto their backs
for a belly rub.
Most here don't enter people spaces,
waiting out there instead
for our love.

Ecstasy of wonder,
the tap tap
tap tap
tap
red sand falling

like calm windless rain
onto a mandala being
born for days,
awareness slows pace,
builds a house of gods
until the time will come
to blow it into
non-existence,

gather the sand,
chant into full emptiness.

I arch up
see the sun
think I've seen this
before
I've said hello for long years,
discard what's old,
make what's new.

He sits next to me
tender
while I cry
in silence
in not understanding,

lets me not understand
and holds my hand
on a concrete step
over a cliff

on a road that takes
His Holiness from
here to the world
and back again.

I can't reach
what beats-down inside.
This self-spin
dance, too, hides
everyone else.

8:05 a.m.
Monks sway, reading and chanting prayer
on shiny wooden floors, dark wine red and orange.
The sand mandala lies covered.
The monks ring bells
clang drums,
resume chanting.
The mandala will soon
be gone.

~~~OOO~~~

8:10 a.m.
I don't know
the murals around me.
Monsters, demons and color.
They evoke dark gloried galaxies
I have to slip somewhere else to enter
the way a new friend takes me
to Seventies Montreal,
warm Sunday mornings,
wood-paneled walls
and the Neverland forests
of my nocturnal voyages.

~~~OOO~~~

You've come awake,
a soft, fragile flower,
no, a poem,
swimming low tide
the kind of waves
that don't threaten with
violence or turmoil
but rest, wait, play--
       yes, even stillness.
So we have started
seeing together.

We can imagine
the branches have
merged with the sky,
new leaves might be waiting
to catch the next morning's dew.
It's a beautiful sight.
I see the pine,
still a thing

apart.

Soon I will touch it,
form with its form,
the monkeys in the forest
won't
catch me.

There you are
sitting, quiet,
eyes closed,
next to the others
we're all under
the blanket
of my mind.

~~~OOO~~~

Jack Kerouac on
Desolation Peak, looking
down, watching,
eating out of tin cans,
doing things feverishly, writing,
thinking about God.

In the Himalayan mountains
thunder rolls, lightning flashes low
and we sit in our room,
watching the rain
fall over McLeod Ganj
making rice porridge
and now I see it,
his self-same God –
hovers around our Hindu shrine outside.

~~~OOO~~~

You are a mountain
and your thoughts are clouds passing by,
our teacher says.
They don't stay.

Outside the window
the briefest sunset,
a hazy pink in soft, upside down-
triangle formation.

The next time I look
the pink is gone.
The clouds are thicker,
becoming one thing,
slowly snaking over
the ridge.

I can't seize the perfections
but it is my only job,
to get there.
What is,
getting there,
in movement,
repose,
sigh it out
to the wind.

Enter rain

before the cold is too much
for the bones,
soak the grass,
make noise on the roof
where the dogs run,
splash the windows

we'll open later
to let the flies out,
when the sky clears and far mountains
return to night.

Red, blue and yellow cloths
hanging from branches, growing out of half a tree.
The other half burned long ago.
The tree tells me:
they'll say it again.
They'll say it again.
We climb to a rock below,
I lie on my stomach,
head in arms,
seeing the mountains
from a cloud.

Say it again
serpent sky,
listen to the water
rushing where there is no water
look what we can be,
witness to a rush of castles
made from hills,
crested with white snow.

The brown baby goat came

to be my friend
let me nuzzle him —

came forward to
press into my thigh,
my underarm,

we held each other
over the ghosts
covered in sage and grass.

Snow
longs to stay,
stretches like granite
along the grassy incline
a trickle of water
hidden
makes a sound like
fairies laughing.
Why wouldn't they laugh?
There's nothing but
clean air and
water here.

Where days fall between climbing
and descending.
Making a clean room,
smelling cinnamon
in my coffee cup,
and drying my purple socks
in the morning sun —
book half open.

Music falls on
stone ruins
yellow from the day.
The sounds reverberate
off carvings,
pouring through the
spaces
between images
of gods.
Horses rising
lovers enmeshed in carnal
depiction.

Architectures of
passion.

My mind throws pieces at me
sometimes slow, like a dance,
other times faster,
more violent
so I don't know
how to defend myself.
Now I see.
Every thought I
don't keep
is one piece of
darkness
in the world removed.

A pot of chai is boiling; bubbles arise.
We sit on a bench
with a pink plastic jug
across from a Ganesh calendar –
I look again,
and no,
it's Hanuman, the monkey –
the ad on top reads
PREETI SPORTS AND
STATIONERS: Kotwali
Bazar, conjuring faint,
dusty things from
gold-laced centuries.

Walking on light,
it's the chair
looking
at the tree. *Not me.*
Sometimes I wish I were
sitting
in my best friend's upstairs den,
watching
the Miss Universe Pageant,
eating
Cool Ranch chips,
like we used to.

I think the flies might be little Buddhas,
buzzing
around
our heads
as we try to meditate
but think of other things,

landing on my nose
as I try in vain
to find my breath,
leaving in silence as
calm regains.

~~~OOO~~~

The Tibetan girl in front of me
in the jeep to Dharamsala
is talking
to her older male friend, with one
of the vehicle's jumps, she bumps her head
on the railing above the window.
She touches her head,
then the railing,
and then her head again,
like she's making a connection,
peace with the cause
of her pain.

~~~OOO~~~

Things To Do Before Leaving Dharamsala:
attend Tenzin Palmo lecture,
go to the dentist,
buy earphones,
and a splitter for the FM radio —
for The Dalai Lama's teaching,
celebrate my birthday,
eat Bhagsu cake,
see Festival films,
have pizza and tsampa porridge,
do retreat,
have chai at the shop,
say goodbye.

~~~OOO~~~

One generation forgets,

leaves
a hole
for their children

to find in themselves,

and they don't know how to fill it

because they don't understand
that it wasn't their hole to fill.

~~~OOO~~~

The heat comes
and the anger is clear,
the sweat gleams
harder,
someone sings,
fills me with gaps inside
my heart: disgust.
Then the heat
subsides,
anger turns
to sadness,
and something has passed,
and something is new.

Cars idle, trying to get by
nuns walking with canes,
prayer
beads.
A knife-sharpening professional
passes with his office –
a bicycle,
and box full of knives.

I imagine samurai
fight to the death in honor.
People cover
their faces from the fumes
with colorful scarves
and robes; monks
book buses and trains
at an agency nearby.

I still don't know,
which passport
do the Tibetans carry?
Postscript: none.
Some have
identity certificates,
but don't belong
to any country.

~~~OOO~~~

I can't get Krishna Das
out of my head,
the way he hardly opens
his mouth and emits the sounds of pure love
and devotion
into a space
in which he has found
his way to peace,
and
how the gods
hear him back.

They say,
use your mind
to control
your mind.
Logicians might say,
this is impossible,
to go within
from within,
but this is what we have
to work with,
        and it's bound
to take us
far.

It is important to study,
we hear on the FM
radio, emitting the sound
of the Dalai Lama
and its English translation.

The voice on the radio
sounds far away.
Much closer,
live and above us,
the sound of His Holiness's laugh,
which booms in
giggling joy.

A young Tibetan mother
holds her baby next to us;
the baby is quiet,
stares at everything.
An older woman sits
on a cushion on a tree stump
while her son leaves in search of the right radio
frequency.
We lean against a railing,
realize we forgot to bring our metallic cups
as monks pass by,
offering butter tea.

A village in a village
in the mountain onto which roads have been built
long ago, but with consideration
for the trees which grow up from old ground
we can only imagine now,
little networks
of insects, worms and life-
giving earth forming the
subterranean city that,
were we to visit,
might appeal to us,
stay awhile.

I remember reading a book
when I was little,
a blue shiny book, about how babies are made
and why we are born,
but nobody talks this clearly
about how to make
happiness
or keep the joys
we find so easily as children,
how to find self-
knowing joy.

My mind winds in-
to places I still can't follow. I awaken to this.
It moves so fast
I don't have time
to find my dreams.
In the half-light of new day, I see the pines
and close my eyes,
scanning for peace, feeling mind-movement
like frogs in a small clear-pond.

I read about Bodhicitta,
how developing a good heart
and feeling compassion for others
is the path to enlightenment,
how every mantra,
prostration
            and action should
be practiced with the intention
to benefit others.
I put the book down and go for a walk
down the mountain, and come
upon the house of a nun,
snug in an enclave,
and there she is chanting mantras
while doing her chores in the tree-
filtered sun.

The head brims,
the heart – I don't know
yet, I have never felt it so full.
It spills over, in sympathy?
Empathy? Compassion?
Universal love?
But these
new visions,
connecting
to where I used to be,
sparkle, filling the air
between leaves,
attracting
each other;
they seem to
whisper through my mind.

      I stifle
my creativity

before my heart can
flow freely. My heart,
which can't flow
like this, stops
in other parts of my body,
trying to make me free.

~~~OOO~~~

One foot down
in front of the other,
sensations under foot
maybe half the time. I don't know where I am,
mostly.
A cat approaches
on the walking path.
Moments later, I'm
hardly there
as I coo and pet her.
I come back, and see
bright trees and setting sun,
feel warmth and softness under my hand.

The monks are in
the Gompa, prayer hall, chanting
and praying for the happiness
of all beings, here
and now, past and future, all
over the universe.
I sit right outside
on a stretch of grass
where I can hear the bells clang,
and ringing sounds of salutation,
the outward and audible
movement of their hearts.

~~~OOO~~~

I make a list
of all the circumstances of my life
to help me see
what I have,
who I am,
what I have done
before to bring me here.

How good it is —
(now I hear him sweeping
the ground
in front of the Medicine Gompa).

~~~OOO~~~

Feeling in sharing
laughing in knowing,
telling stories
until the

gong

tells us
to return
to silence.

Native American shamans,
I tell my new friends

when silence breaks,

came to us
        in this seeing,
to my partner in life and I, under a redwood tree
in California, and began a healing dance
that brought sick people from all over
to gather together under the tree,
guiding me to seek knowledge
of magic and Life.

A shadow passes over a spider web
and disappears,
but one flicker
from the sun's rays and a perfect formation appears.
        It sways in
and out
        of view. The same, too,
of my words which have harmed others,
        which can't be
seen or heard now,
        that cause every violence.

~~~OOO~~~

A layer of film forms at the top of my glass of chai.

We meditate: a light
comes to sit on top of my head.

Covering? Protecting?
Loving?

It descends
and dissolves
into me, but the white
light I am led to be filled
with is a murky grey,
because I am still afraid
of what cannot be divided.

Wandering everywhere
but where I am,
others go for walks in the forest,
recite incantations,
learn-feel-be,
around me.
We try,
as we keep quiet, to
feel ourselves in
presence.

I don't think I lost my self when I was instructed to
go looking.
I also couldn't find it.
This didn't make me
happy or sad, or even
equanimous.

Yet everything
remains.

"A moment
with your beloved
and the river
changes its course,"
says the text
on the page thrust in front of me
as I walk
very slowly
around the Gompa
        in walking meditation.
Monkeys and ants
visit too.

She closes the book
and walks away
with a smile.

A red-robed monk
in the distance
in the forest
not far from our
retreat grounds,
sitting,
hands on knees,
meditating during the
auspicious time when
day turns to dusk.
Tea is prepared
the world falls
dusk.

The air turns monsoon now. We fly around
looking for an ATM machine
that has funds in it,
        dust flying everywhere,
chips and cookies
bags on the ground, cars honking in loud
conversation, it starts to rain,
buses logjam,
eggplant and okra lie
on rucksacks on the street,
we're down
from the mountain in the Indian plains.

~~~OOO~~~

"Love is never die."
"This is a Frist love Letter."
"Life is short."
"Don't break my heart."
"Don't touch
my Frist heart."
"Nobody love me."
"The best momo
in India."

~~~OOO~~~

This is the magic,
finding a girl
who reminds me
of cardigan sweaters.
That color I can't name.
It was all over
my childhood
friend's basement.

Radiohead, playing
now in the Magic Tree
Café, from OK Computer
the album
of my first
relationship
with love.

It's a familiar site now,
cows resting on hay,
munching idly on grass,
sniffing for food,
young ones nearby.
A bucket of scraps
descend close to the cow's flaring nostrils,
which snuff as her head lowers
and pokes around, swallowing banana peels whole,
considering mango pits,
filling her belly
of worship.

~~~OOO~~~

Banoffie pie at midnight
as Spain crushes Italy in
the Euro Cup final. No one cheers loudly,
people sleep in
guesthouses
nearby in the
thin air,
moods lift and fall,
locals drink beer and
liquor now, weed grows
on the side of the road.
The night disappears
into a cloud.

Stomping on dust,
cracked feet, naked bodies,
the feel of the air is bright yellow, orange and red,
even now at night, rain has started
to fall, beating drums
thrum louder,
more rhythmic,
chanting turns to wailing,
the hour darkens
but the white lights of a festival filter
into weightless sleep.

There's a logjam
on the road to Keylong.
A chai wallah
sells tea and coffee.
We're with the clouds now, 3000 meters or more.
Our bag of chips bloated
to burst, wet clothes
from this morning's rain
hang on the railing of the our seat
to dry, the driver tries to make a sharp turn
in the mud.
Stalled in
Himachal.

~~~OOO~~~

Sit down,
there's a red plastic chair waiting.
It has old paint stains on it
and it has many friends just like it.
There's a design
of flowers and mountains
on the sides of the beige
plastic tables sitting
at the edge of the world, overhanging
a drop
          to the very bottom,
from where you can squint in the sun and see snow-
crested peaks emerge from misty clouds floating
beneath.

~~~OOO~~~

Stalled,
we wait in a valley,
barracks
dwarfed
by the Himalayan foothills. There are no bigger
spaces.
I see another Truth: the enormity of making
a connection
with someone,
looking in their eyes,
seeing orbits in one shared smile.

Sky temple,
future Buddha Maitreya looks off into the distance
surrounded by the 35
forms of Buddha.
Sun comes in
shining special
into a room full of money and burning
oil offerings, and tomorrow-
type predictions.

From the sky down, a town half green,
half desert,
where the glaciers do not melt.
You can't see the bustle from
here, the life. Soon Muslim
prayers begin, incantations
through loudspeakers past
the town, up into the sky
that covers everything
without weight.

The sky extends to Sea visions.
Prayers reach to
Spirit.

~~~OOO~~~

"Choosing one religion over another creates

    separation,"

the monk tells us.
He writes fairy tales and plays music too.
He's built temples around the world.
"To concentrate on books
or driving is easy," he says,
"to focus on meditation is more
difficult. Don't do it for
selfish purposes. Practice karma
yoga to serve others,
and the concentration
will come."

"Knowledge and wisdom
are like
oil on water," he continues.
"They don't mix.
Remove knowledge,
and space for wisdom
becomes possible."
His eyes shine in
the late-afternoon light.

~~~OOO~~~

Ladakh is the seat of the world
the music
it makes
is the physical form of us

deep-
down,
          the sounds meet with us,
and retreat
and we try not to run screaming
to find them again.

LUNCH + DINNER
On first day
+
Snakes
With
Tea:
HEMIS FESTIVAL
Special Package,
29/30-06.

~~~OOO~~~

Thiksey, Shey,
Spituk, Matho,
each with a temple on a hill,
        with a river and grass and trees on one side,
barren on the other.

Rich browns
and greens from the water,
and sandy, rusty color
under rainless
sky.

I've come here.
Across towns and rivers,
oceans,
highways,
clashed with Hindu gods,
eaten Kashmiri bread,
learned that Avalokiteshvara
is the Buddhist God of Compassion.
A
melting
takes
place,
into physical
sense.

~~~OOO~~~

Words can be so simple,
talk of things
like black and white,
sun and sky,
grey and faith,
until you hear songs in another language or read
poetry filled with words
strung together to form
dark dramatic mazes
      Why not reach for sounds the body knows
how to laugh and cry with?

~~~OOO~~~

Like a tenement cigarette
motel, the word
Manali hanging off the side
of the building in bright
yellow and red.
So much yellow and red
here, the monks flapping
their robes over
rounded shoulders,
the Windhorses,

      flags waving in the white
wind.

~~~OOO~~~

Loud night noises,
a television blaring news
and dance competitions,
a burnt rug soaking with water
from the neighbor's toilet, huddled close on
a good hard bed, hearing
chai drinkers effusing outside
the window, Hindu
festivals on every side.
Drums don't clash with
but invite silence.
Everything here joins
everything else.

~~~OOO~~~

The first time
I saw
a bag of
Mad Angles chips
lying flattened
on the road,
I thought it
said
Mad Angels
(Jack).

The Ganges flows over onto the boardwalk
and recedes,
leaving spectacles
of food and ghosts
of past offerings
on the ground.

        The Ganga moves-silky,
south, strong,
my emotions
don't know
where to go.

A row of sadhus,
(orange-clad, seeking)
sit listless, strung
along walls
and on concrete benches
sinking into the ground
next to mango orchards
lying in wait
for next
season.
"Hari Om," they say
as we pass by.

~~~OOO~~~

It's easy to feel
the dream of everything
here, where the Ganga drifts
by underneath our bamboo floor
with its mesh of colors strewn across
like jewels, over there the bridge rocks
silently under
the weight
of family
photo takers,
monkeys eating
chicken, cows clomping by,
motorbikes honking
for passage Through.

A mango for every
prophesy,
a vision for his rheumy
eyes,
calls out
"Fortune! Fortune!"
The bird waits for
his turn
at the cards,
"Your future!" He
says, smiling.

~~~OOO~~~

I am looking for the way out of Time.
It's a jungle in there.
I want
and need
and cry
out in misery there. I cannot expel
the poisons. On the way out,
the strains
of *Wizard of Oz*,
old favorite,
a real cine-
vision, Ajna-tale, Third Eye,
the great Sage-
fool.

~~~OOO~~~

The ant carries half his weight
in front of him, a huge morsel of food
that fell
from my napkin
as I wiped my hands
after eating,
the flies will take one
crystal of sugar
if they don't
drown in the chai.

I see a body made
of tiny red
smiles
embedded in little white
circles,
this is my body.
The Ganga is swift
outside. The Brahman chants
below.
Then my body breaks,
sonorous dissolution.

A door: thick, wooden,
with etchings and reliefs
from a culture I
can't place at first, until
I hear music from
Renaissance Italy,
still and graceful
for the Courts.
This is the heavy
door I see,
opening in the middle,
to lands far
from here.

The paint is speaking
from this century,
thanking
gurus,
The Beatles,
everything that
made Love
here and Be Still,
the ashram sings.

A perfect yellow
leaf has death
            immanent
on the left side.
            Still it curves
                    majestic,
            it won't crumble,
the walls
are not undying,
but still
I can look
through them
after forty years.

~~~OOO~~~

Say it again.
There's an entrance.
Will you
arrive, and what
will you see? The body
moves and the river
falls
over rocks,
carries
secrets and prayers
going by.
But we
can only see the
body, mistake stillness for gravity.

At Haridwar, the Ganges breaks away
from the Himalayas
and begins.
Pilgrims flood daily.
Piles and piles of shoes
gather at a stall,
people find their
spot at the steps of the ghats,
find ways of changing into
trunks hidden, in full view,
snap photos in the Holy water.

A woman,
maybe ten years younger than me,
has her whole family
dressed in purple.
Her face is sharp and small
and narrow, like mine. Her
eyes and smile are luminous.

She tries to put back together
the pieces of plastic toys
with a screaming baby,
shaved for Krishna Day,
or the Ganga,
        by her side,
her other daughter,
an exact replica of her,
helping throughout.

Early morning Delhi, chai chai chaiiiii coffee,
the wallahs
never drop their wares on the moving train.
Families wake up, lit by the first
sun like Vermeer's
meticulous subjects,
and smile as they gather
their things.

~~~OOO~~~

A train sleeps.
Cloth from home turns
seats into furniture,
three hours late,
meals behind,
face carved
with seat lines,
daylight still arrives
on schedule.

I call
your face
and it appears in full
clarity,
but it's your eyes
I see first,
how they are
so large
from taking so much of the world into them,
and how
they see into mine,
not here,
not to my person,
somewhere through
to where I cry
out for you.

~~~OOO~~~

First a feeling
and then the parts emerge;
the way the song invokes
a whole decade of life,
how they chose purple
cushions and an orange tablecloth
and how I love those
colors, standing out in the clutter of a café space;
how yesterday
we bore witness
to a body burning up into the Ganga sky.

The Buddha of Compassion's
arms spread
out a thousand times
in the shape of a perfect round tree I photographed
a few months ago.
When I imagine one
now the other
immediately arises in my view
of how things are
in a world
of kindness
and right seeing.

~~~OOO~~~

Puja.
Unceasing creation.
Paper and fire offered
with song and devotion
onto Ganga's great arms.
Every night is like this.
Flower gods swim down
current. Occasionally, a
silence where sky meets
river. Below us,
an artist draws a young
boy serving chai
long after sunset,
who turns to look at
his evolving image.
He leaves his stall
and barrels up the
steps to pose, serious,
still, confident. A boat
passes behind all this, a lone
traveler in his floating castle,
lit with Christmas lights and
all this grace.

I Used to Dream of Here

          A movement
takes place,
not from up there
or through contours and angles.
It comes, forges
right through
to love-marked time.

It strikes me
as I look at the water
streaming
over Zen rocks:
the sound is everywhere
          I have been that matters.

Quietly spoken words are white
dreams unfurling old dragon breath
onto grass, between mountains rising up,
spirits of something in gentle observance.

~~~OOO~~~

To me it seems now
that a flower
is not from ground or sky,
        has no sides,
there is no walking around
looking for nascence.
I have been missing
everything
and still
you stay.

~~~OOO~~~

There is nothing here.
They took the town away.
Mountainous remains,
it's time we go.

~~~OOO~~~

My finger slips
and I am now part of this borrowed (wall)
until the (   )
itself
disappears,
after a long decoration.

I sit
in a tiny kitchen
and can't shake the fact of many other kitchen minds.
I want to stop
to go,
            embark
on this visit,
                        reach out for them,
lose them
in one final act
of kitchen defiance.

Be where you are.
The memory of the
sun's recent emergence,
how many times I talk
about the mountains that
move too, if more slowly,
on this unfolding island
that might float away
forever, where
I heard 'morning'
for the first time
in eight months.

Show me a rock,
and I will
look around for the way
             fallen branches
are still wet under
tall cedars,
and come back to it,
wanting only to
search for its god.

I struggle to hold a mind
that has half
left this world already,
just for now.
Once I fought to join it,
and then to meet
all the others swimming
inside, and now I see it
on young faces,
a new mind now. I
don't recognize it.
I'm still
       fighting
with my own.

I want a lost art
like moving in sand
singing the blossoms alive.

The king of the house
stands in the long shadow
of the mountain, that
has not swallowed the house
        yet. He can't see the mountain
from inside,
        at best has a view
of grass coming
        into spring
and a few solid tree trunks
marking
the entrance
of the dark and
        deep forest. But every
morning he
drops
to his knees
and gives thanks,
        and the mountain comes to him.
They are reacquainted
in the cold
pre-dawn morning

before one has rice and tea
and the other continues with
the business of being.
I can see the house with the red roof, I have
never met the king, and the mountain comes back
in another dream.

Cedar trees now, who knows what temple on top.
Cars drive
by the house,
small and shiny, out of my view. Then a train.
My head hurts
from too much movement.

I even imagine the mountain taunting
me, and become angry
at my own stupidity. Every time I look, the trees
      play still in the sun. Like the trees,
I am
still,
sun-facing,
breathing its life
too. My life
comes and goes.
The curtains bore me.
The photograph makes me
want to
visit places where
I can grow flowers
in my head.

In the Bamboo Talking (Haiku)

ever-moving clouds
obscure full moon
still, deep, shiver

the stone won't cut
pebbles stop growing
side by side laughing

dark night falls
everything thought wrong,
still, i need you

twilight takes me
secret worlds laced-in
fairies and roses

new winter beckons
clarity sweeps
lighter than wind

cognizance — gift
we take
before dawn

i would like nothing
more than hear
your mountain story

forest dwelling
tree bottom
felled with compassion

we move time
a deity
forever breath

morning fog
carved persimmon tree
sky, crooked and black

guess *(i won't)*
how many spirits pass
this sacred hall

we resist
the dance, the world
spins chaos

snow wondrous
temples hiding
sacred ground

inside the mountain,
a lonely highway,
missing light and hue

leaf strewn decks,
wind subtle,
recreate divine

grave clusters
roadside
reminiscences

rice, sweetened carrots,
grated daikon, hot
soup, breakfast heart.

in japanese (kokoro)
the same word
heart and mind

kokoro
the field arises
old, naked emotion

kokoro
we don't think our way,
heart-of-songs

quiet wife
aging beauty
incense worships

hot street-front
wailing mosque-
india floods back.

why welcome
the sun, gaze at the moon,
shake under clouds?

ladybug robes
the same color —
the dalai lama

make the trip
with the windhorse
gods fluttering close

come to whisper
silences to thick glass
cold in breath.

window mountains
roar. i too
in soft reflection

Lightning Source UK Ltd.
Milton Keynes UK
UKOW06f2347230216

268947UK00008B/144/P